CIVILIZATIONS PAST TO PRESENT

GREECE

D1398718

KEVIN SUPPLES

PICTURE CREDITS:
Cover Peter Poulides/Stone; pages 3 (top), 7 David S. Boyer/National
Geographic Society, Image Collection (NGSIC); pages 3 (bottom), 15
(bottom) Attic red-figure amphora by the Berlin Painter. c. 490/480
B.C. Athene/Herakles. Antikenmuseum Basel und Sammlung Ludwig,
inv. no. BS 456; pages 4-5 John M. Thompson/NGSIC; page 8 Todd
Gipstein/NGSIC; pages 9, 11 H.M. Herget/NGSIC; page 10 Photodisc;
pages 12-13 Robert C. Magis/NGSIC; page 13 Ira Block/NGSIC; page
14 Farrell Grehen/NGSIC; page 15 (top) Hartman Dewitt/Comstock;
page 16 B. Van Being/Image Bank; page 17 Win Parks/NGSIC; page
17 (inset) Michael Kuh/NGSIC; pages 18, 19 (bottom), 23 Erich
Lessing/Art Resource, NY; page 19 (top) F. & H. Schreider/NGSIC;
pages 20-21 Tom Lovell/NGSIC; page 22 © Walter Bibikow/Folio, Inc.;
page 24 James P. Blair/NGSIC; back cover(top to bottom) Sylvain
Grandadam/Stone, Attic red-figure amphora by the Berlin Painter. c.
490/480 B.C. Athene/Herakles. Antikenmuseum Basel und Sammlung
Ludwig, inv. no. BS 456, Photodisc, D. E. Cox/Stone, Photodisc

Cover: Athens, Greece

Contents page: The Acropolis, Greek vase

MAPS
Equator Graphics

Produced through the worldwide resources of the National Geographic
Society, John M. Fahey, Jr., President and Chief Executive Officer;
Gilbert M. Grosvenor, Chairman of the Board; Nina D. Hoffman,
Executive Vice President and President, Books and School Publishing.

PREPARED BY NATIONAL GEOGRAPHIC SCHOOL PUBLISHING
Ericka Markman, Vice President; Steve Mico, Editorial Director;
Marianne Hiland, Editorial Manager; Anita Schwartz, Project Editor;
Tara Peterson, Editorial Assistant; Jim Hiscott, Design Manager; Linda
McKnight, Art Director; Diana Bourdrez, Anne Whittle, Photo Research;
Matt Wascavage, Manager of Publishing Services; Sean Philpotts,
Production Coordinator.

Production: Clifton M. Brown III, Manufacturing and Quality Control.

PROGRAM DEVELOPMENT
Gare Thompson Associates, Inc.

BOOK DESIGN
3r1 Group

Published by the National Geographic Society
1145 17th Street, N.W.
Washington, D.C. 20036-4688

ISBN: 0-7922-8673-1

Third Printing February, 2002
Printed in Canada.

CONTENTS

INTRODUCTION

Imagine wearing the same clothes as your parents or playing games with dried bones. Imagine taking a bath in olive oil or going to a play with 10,000 other people. These are some of the things that you would do if you lived long ago in **ancient** Greece.

Greece is a country in southern Europe. It is mountainous and dry. Greece also has many islands and **ports**, places where ships come and go. A main city we will visit is Athens. So let's go back in time 2,500 years. You will see just how different Greece of long ago was from Greece today.

GREECE: THEN AND NOW

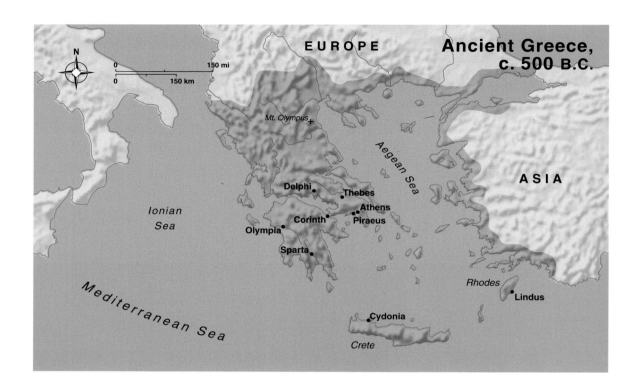

Ancient Greece, c. 500 B.C.

Ancient Greece was a great civilization of long ago. Drama, poetry, art, and science were important to its people. Many of their arts and ideas are still important to us today.

Ancient Greece was a group of small settlements called city-states. By 500 B.C., many city-states had developed on the mainland and islands of Greece. Each city-state had its own laws, customs, and leaders.

Two of the largest and most important city-states were Athens and Sparta. Athens was known for its beautiful buildings, statues, plays, and democratic government. Athens was not ruled by a king or queen. Its citizens ran the city-state. The citizens voted on important issues, such as whether to go to war or how much to pay in taxes. Sparta was known for its armies and warlike character. Athens and Sparta were often at war with each other.

Greece Today

N

0   150 mi
0   150 km

Thessaloniki

Mt. Olympus +

Aegean Sea

TURKEY

Ionian Sea

Thebes

Corinth Athens
Piraeus

Sparta

Rhodes
Lindos

Mediterranean Sea

Crete

Look at the map of ancient Greece on page 6. Can you find Athens and Sparta? Which city-state lies closest to the sea? What other city-states do you see?

Now compare the maps of ancient and modern Greece. How are ancient and modern Greece alike and different? Why do you think the people of Greece have always turned to the sea for trade and travel?

WORD POWER

The word *democracy* comes from two Greek words—*demos,* meaning "the common people," and *kratos,* meaning "power." Democracy means that the power to rule comes from the people.

HOUSES

In ancient Greece, most houses were made of dried mud bricks. The roof was made of tiles. The floor was dirt and covered with rugs. On the walls hung brightly colored hangings woven by the women of the house. Greek houses had few, tiny windows. During the day the house was hot inside.

In the center of the house was the courtyard. This open space did not have a roof. It was cooler than the house. The courtyard was like a family room. It was a place where everyone spent time together. Families washed their clothes, cooked, and ate their food there. In the evenings they played games and relaxed in their courtyards.

Today, houses in Greece look much like the houses of ancient Greece. But they are different in some ways. Today's houses have lots of windows. Many are air conditioned. In the cities, you see many kinds of houses and apartment buildings. Some modern houses by the sea have huge glass walls with a view of the sea.

Housing on this Greek island is a blend of the old and new.

LOOKING BACK

Ancient Greek houses had thick mud walls and few windows. Robbers broke in by digging their way through the wall of a house! They were called "wall-diggers"!

CLOTHES

Greece has hot, dry summers and mild, wet winters. **In ancient Greece**, how did the people dress to stay cool? In summer, Greek men and women wore loosely draped clothes made of linen. The linen clothes felt cool in the heat. When the weather was cooler, they wore wool.

Men, women, and children wore clothes that looked much the same. Everyone wore **tunics**, a loose-fitting kind of dress, gathered at the waist with a belt. Women usually wore their tunics ankle length, while children wore theirs shorter. Men usually wore long tunics every day and shorter ones for hunting.

Some people wore big cloaks over their tunics. Their clothes were brightly colored in reds, purples, pinks, and yellows. Most people wore sandals.

Today, Greek men, women, and children wear the same clothes as you do. However, for special festivals and holidays, they often wear clothes that look like those worn in ancient Greece. And, of course, everyone wears sandals in the summer!

Workmen usually wore short tunics so that they could move around easily.

FOOD

Have you ever eaten Greek food? If so, you probably have eaten many of the same dishes that the ancient Greeks ate. **In ancient Greece,** people ate bread, olives, figs, goat cheese, and fish. They did not eat much meat. Meat was for special occasions. Mostly, they ate fish and vegetables. Figs and olives grew well in the hot, dry climate. Goats and sheep could graze on the dry hillsides. Fish were always available from the waters along Greece's long coastline.

The ancient Greeks cooked their food over open fires. They used honey to sweeten food. Goat's milk was a popular drink with meals.

Today, the Greeks still eat fish from the Mediterranean Sea and cook their food in olive oil. People around the world enjoy eating Greek food. Greek dishes often include lamb. A popular dish is Greek salad made with olives, feta cheese, tomatoes, onions, and an olive oil and vinegar dressing. Another popular Greek dish eaten today is baklava. This is a sweet dessert made with honey and nuts.

Many traditional Greek foods are enjoyed today.

LOOKING BACK

The ancient Greeks ate with their hands or used a knife or spoon. There were no forks! Sometimes they kept bowls of olive oil or water on the table so they could rinse their fingers as they ate.

In addition to reading, writing, and mathematics, Greek students were taught music, poetry, sports, and debate.

SCHOOL

In ancient Greece, only boys could go to school. Often, only boys from wealthy families could afford to go to school. Poorer children had to work. Boys who did go to school started at seven years old. They studied mathematics, poetry, music, and athletics. Athletics was as important in ancient Greece as reading and writing. Classes were often small, with only seven or eight students in a class.

Some girls learned to read and write, but most girls helped at home. At 12 years old, boys and girls were thought of as adults. They brought their toys to a temple and left them there. Girls often married the next year, when they were 13.

Today, all Greek children go to school. School is free. Elementary school goes through the sixth grade, followed by six years of high school. Students must go to school until they are 15. Then they decide whether to continue or to leave school and learn a job.

LOOKING BACK

In ancient Greece, students wrote on wax tablets. They reused these tablets. They wrote on them with a stylus, or bronze tool. The stylus looks like a pen.

FARMING

In ancient Greece, many people were farmers. As the early morning sun beat down on their fields, the farmers began to work. The land was dry and rocky. In summer, there was little water for crops. By the end of the day, the farmers' white clothes were dusty and dirty.

Farmers grew wheat, beans, and fruit. Some kept bees to make honey. They used donkeys to help them plow their fields. Many farmers kept sheep and goats, too. Sheep provided wool for clothes. Goats gave the farmers milk and cheese.

Two important crops that farmers grew were olives and grapes. People made wine and raisins from the grapes. They made olive oil from the olives. Ancient Greeks used olive oil for washing, lighting lamps, and cooking.

Today, farming in Greece is much like it was in ancient times. Olives and grapes are still important crops. Some farmers still use donkeys to plow just as they did long ago. But now some farmers keep track of their crops on computers and sell their products on the Internet.

LOOKING BACK

Olive trees were special in ancient Greece. People believed they were a gift from the gods. Anyone caught killing an olive tree was put to death. Today, olive branches are a symbol of peace.

THE AGORA

In ancient Greece, farmers with extra crops took them to the agora, or marketplace. There they sold their crops in stalls. Each town in ancient Greece had an agora.

The agora was a place to buy many different kinds of goods, such as sandals, dishes, and cloth. The agora was also a place for people to get together. People rested, ate, and watched the entertainment. Sword-swallowers, acrobats, and magicians performed. People also told riddles. Riddles were very popular in ancient Greece.

Today, many towns in Greece still have agoras. People have stalls and sell many different things, such as jewelry, pottery, clothes, and food. Have you ever been to a farmers' market? The farmers' markets of today are like the old Greek agoras.

You can buy different kinds of olives and other foods in farmers' markets in Greece today.

TRADE

What if you lived at the edge of the sea? How could you make a living? **In ancient Greece**, many people sailed ships and traded goods. Ships carried goods such as olive oil, grapes, and figs back and forth to other lands.

Greece is so mountainous that sailing from one place to another is easier than traveling over land. Imagine sailing across the sea in a wooden ship. You have to be careful not to hit any rocks. You also have to watch out for pirates.

Today, Greece has many port cities. Shipping is still an important industry. One port city is Piraeus. Piraeus is one of the largest ports on the Mediterranean Sea. It's a busy place—full of fishing boats, ferries, and cruise ships. Today, many people in Greece work on ships.

LOOKING BACK

Pirates in ancient times carried a battering ram, or heavy wooden beam, on their ships. They battered, or hit, merchant ships until they began to sink. Then they took all their goods.

Fishing boats dock at Piraeus, an important Greek port today and in ancient times.

Statues of women were used as columns to support the roof of this Greek temple.

ART

The ancient Greeks created different kinds of art. They made statues to honor their gods and heroes. Many artists carved their statues out of marble. Other artists used ivory, gold, and silver to make jewelry. However, the ancient Greeks did not have art in their homes. Artists made statues just for public places and temples.

Many beautiful pieces of pottery were created by the artists of ancient Greece. The artists liked to use vases to tell stories. They would decorate their vases with stories about ancient Greek heroes or gods.

The pottery that the ancient Greeks used every day had different shapes and designs. There were bowls, jugs, drinking goblets, and bottles to hold perfume. Today, you can see many Greek vases and other pieces of art in museums.

15

The Parthenon is made from white marble. Today, only ruins of this ancient Greek temple remain.

ARCHITECTURE

Ancient Greece was noted for its architecture. One of the most famous buildings is the Parthenon, meaning "the house of the maiden." We can still visit it today. It stands on a hill called the Acropolis which overlooks the city of Athens. The Parthenon was built to honor the goddess Athena. It is more than 2,000 years old!

Today, many public buildings, such as banks and libraries, have columns and entrances like ancient Greek temples. If you look around your own community, you may see buildings that look like the ones in ancient Greece. Does the building have columns? Most of the temples in ancient Greece had columns. The columns were at the entrance of the temples.

Perhaps your community has a statue of a famous hero in a park or in front of a public building. When you look at the statue, think of the ancient Greeks. They created beautiful statues to honor their gods and heroes.

PLAYS

In ancient Greece, people loved to tell stories. They often went to see plays. Some theaters could hold over 10,000 people! Many were built on hillsides so everyone could see the stage.

Ancient Greeks watched plays only during the daytime. They sometimes watched three or four plays in a day. Then they voted for the one they liked best. Instead of clapping, people whistled and stamped their feet to show how much they liked it.

The ancient Greeks even had special effects in their plays. For thunder they used pebbles rolled on a copper sheet. Sometimes they used cranes to lift the actors. A favorite ending for Greek plays was to have the gods come down from the sky to solve the characters' problems.

Today, many of our plays are based on themes and characters from ancient Greek plays. We go to the theater at night and also during the day.

This ancient Greek theater is still used today. It seats as many as 14,000.

17

DELPHI

In ancient Greece, many people came to Delphi to visit the temple of the god Apollo. An oracle, or a person who told the future, was there. People came to ask the oracle questions. A priestess gave them answers. Delphi became very famous. People believed it was the center of the world.

The ancient Greeks also held athletic games to honor the gods. These sports events were called "the crown games." The games at Delphi honored the god Apollo.

LOOKING BACK

Children often played a game called knucklebones. They used dried animal bones to play it. The game is like jacks. The object is to pick up and hold as many bones as possible without dropping them.

Each winner received a crown, or wreath, usually made of olive leaves. Some of the events were running, chariot racing, boxing, wrestling, and jumping.

Delphi is one of the most popular tourist attractions in Greece today.

The ancient stadium at Delphi is near the top of a hill. It's shaped like the letter U. It held about 7,000 people. People sat on the hillside to watch the games.

Today, people visit the beautiful ruins of Delphi. They climb the hills to see the temples that the ancient people built. They watch the sun rise over the hills, lighting the temple ruins.

MEET APOLLO

Apollo was the god of oracles, music, and light. People asked Apollo to bring them good crops. Apollo also stood for justice. He was famous for never telling a lie. Sometimes the sun was called "Apollo's chariot." The first spacecraft to land people on the moon, *Apollo 11,* was named after this Greek god.

OLYMPIC GAMES

Olympia was another city-state that held important crown games. The games at Olympia, called the Olympic Games, honored Zeus, the king of the gods.

In ancient Greece, these games took place every four summers. People from all the city-states came to the games. Some came to compete. Others came to watch. While the games were played, wars stopped. No one wanted to miss the games!

The first games were in 776 B.C. The games lasted for five days. One of the games was called *pankration*. It was a cross between boxing and wrestling. Anything could happen. The only thing not allowed in this game was eye-gouging. It sounds like modern wrestling on television.

When winners of the games went back home, towns honored them with cash prizes and free meals for life. Unlike today's Olympic Games, there were no prizes for second or third place.

The first modern Olympic Games were held in Athens in 1896. **Today**, many of the ancient sports and games are played in the summer Olympics.

LOOKING BACK

Only men could watch the ancient Greek games at Olympia. But women had their own athletic games at Olympia. These games honored the goddess Hera, the wife of Zeus.

An unusual event in the Olympics was a race in which the runners wore armor.

CONTRIBUTIONS

The ancient Greeks lived a long time ago. But many of their ideas and culture remain with us today. Look around and you will see their gifts to us.

People still study the works of ancient Greek thinkers, artists, and writers. We enjoy plays based on ancient Greek writings.

Across the United States, many banks, libraries, and state capitols look like ancient Greek temples.

Statues honoring our heroes grace our public spaces, just as they did in ancient Greece.

Many English words such as *politics*, *stadium*, and *music* come from the Greek language. And Greek ideas about democracy have spread to countries all over the world. We even continue to have Olympic Games! We have learned a lot from the ancient Greeks.

The Lincoln Memorial in Washington, D.C., looks like the Parthenon in Athens, Greece.

GLOSSARY

agora the marketplace in ancient Greece

ancient very old

architecture the art of planning and designing buildings

citizen a member of a particular community or country who has certain rights and responsibilities

city-state a settlement or city with its own government

civilization a group of people or a country with highly developed farming, trade, government, art, and science

democratic a way of governing a country in which the people choose their leaders

oracle a person who tells the future

port a harbor or place where boats and ships can anchor safely

tunic a loose-fitting kind of dress

Music was an important part of the Greek culture.

INDEX